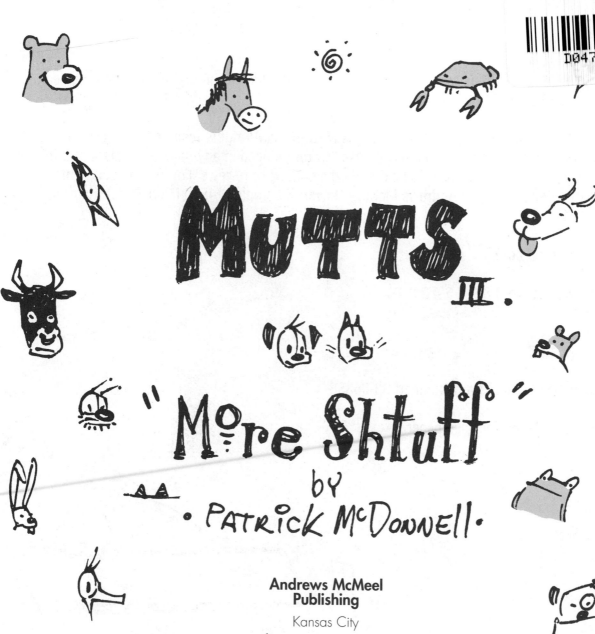

MUTTS III.

"More Shtuff"

by
· PATRICK McDONNELL ·

**Andrews McMeel
Publishing**

Kansas City

D0472972

Mutts is distributed internationally by King Features Syndicate, Inc. For information write King Features Syndicate, Inc., 216 East 45th Street, New York, New York 10017.

More Shtuff: Mutts III copyright © 1998 by Patrick McDonnell. All rights reserved. Printed in the United States of America. No part of this book may be used or reproduced in any manner whatsoever without written permission except in the case of reprints in the context of reviews. For information, write Andrews McMeel Publishing, an Andrews McMeel Universal company, 4520 Main Street, Kansas City, Missouri 64111.

www.andrewsmcmeel.com.

98 99 00 01 02 EBA 10 9 8 7 6 5 4 3 2 1

ISBN: 0-8362-6823-7

Library of Congress Catalog Card Number: 98-85338

More Shtuff is printed on recycled paper.

T?

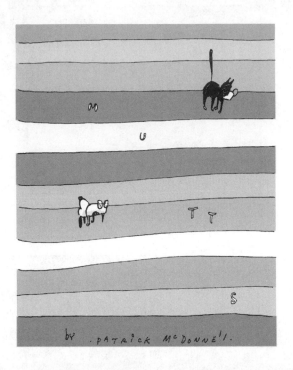

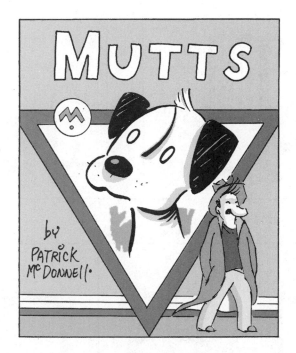

HMMMMM...

MOOCH, YOU'VE BEEN **STARING** AT YOURSELF FOR **HOURS**!!! WHAT'S **WRONG** WITH YOU!?!

NOT MUCH.

GEE, I'M **SO CUTE**... I'M GOING TO GIVE MYSELF A LI'L SHMACK...

MMMM...

OOP.

SMACK

EARL, I LOOKED-SEE AND LOOKED-SEE UNTIL I SAW THE "REAL" ME!

OH... AND HOW DID THE "REAL" YOU LOOK-SEE?

HUNGRY.

22

"THE THINKER"

30

lick lick lick lick lick
lick lick lick lick lick
licklick lick lick lick lick
lick lick lick lick lick
lick lick lick lick
lick lick lick lick lick
lick lick lick
lick

lick lick lick lick lick lick
lick lick lick lick lick lick
lick lick lick lick lick
lick lick lick lick lick
lick lick lick lick
lick lick lick
lick lick
lick

38

41

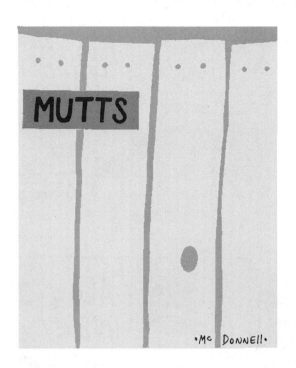

MUTTS
by
Patrick
McDonnell

EARL, IT'S UP TO **YOU** TO RESCUE SHTINKY FROM THIS **WELL**!!! **YOU MUST** BE LIKE LASSIE AND **SAVE** THE DAY!

YOU MUST RUN TO THE TOWNSPEOPLE AND MAKE THEM **UNDERSTAND**!!! BRING BACK **HELP**!!! GO, MY FUZZY FRIEND, **GO!**

WHO'S LASSIE?

I DUNNO.

I **MUST** SAVE SHTINKY. SOMEHOW I MUST MAKE PEOPLES UNDERSTAND **ME**!

BARK BARK ARF.

OH, I KNOW WHAT **YOU** WANT... **WHAT** A SMART DOGGY!

YOU WANT A **NICE BIG** COOKIE!

JEEZ— I SAID **SOMETHING** RIGHT.

MOOCH... I'M SCARED... IT'S DARK DOWN HERE... AND I'M ALL ALONE...

SHTINKY, YOU MUST ALWAYS REMEMBER NO MATTER WHERE YOU ARE, YOU'RE **NEVER** ALONE.

I KNOW...

FLEAS.

THERE'S SHTINKY'S "OZZIE." **HE'LL** UNDERSTAND TO FOLLOW **ME!**

ARF!

EARL... WHAT IS IT?

I'LL SAY IT WITH MY **VOICE**... I'LL SAY IT WITH MY **EYES**... I'LL SAY IT WITH **ALL MY HEART**... I'LL SAY IT...

... WITH HIS **TIE!**

WELL, JULES, YOU SILLY THING!

STUCK DOWN A **DECORATIVE** WELL...

...THAT **YOU** COULD HAVE CLIMBED OUT OF ANY OLD TIME.

WELL?

WHAT D'YA KNOW.

'TWAS NICE TO SEE YA, "SHTINK," BUT WE MUST SAY GOOD-BYE.

OH, EARLY... OH, MOOCHIE... LET'S **NOT** SAY "GOO·BYE" LET'S SAY "YELLO."

YELLO!

GOO·BYE!

HEY! MOOCH, LET'S GO PLAY!

CATS HAVE THEIR OWN AGENDA, THANK YOU.

OH, AND WHAT'S ON YOUR CALENDAR TODAY?

WHAT DAY IS IT?

MONDAY.

MONDAY...

TODAY I LOAF.

AND WHAT'S ON YOUR "CAT AGENDA" TODAY?

TODAY, I LOAF.

WEDNESDAY — LOAF

THURSDAY — LOAF

FRIDAY... — LOAF...

SO EVERY DAY YOU LOAF.

NO, WISE GUY. I DON'T LOAF ON SUNDAY!

WELL, THAT'S GOOD.

SURE. I NEED ONE DAY OFF.

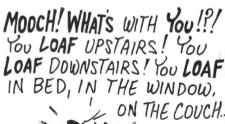

MOOCH! WHAT'S WITH YOU!?! YOU LOAF UPSTAIRS! YOU LOAF DOWNSTAIRS! YOU LOAF IN BED, IN THE WINDOW, ON THE COUCH...

CAT — YOU HAVE A VERY SERIOUS PROBLEM

YOU'RE RIGHT...

I NEED TO SHIMPLIFY MY LIFE

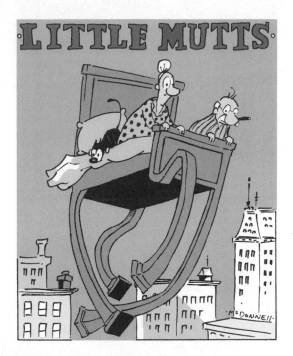

MUTTS.
BY
PATRICK McDONNELL

WHAT A SCENT!

INTRIGUING!

QUITE SUBLIME.

HEY!

EARL! DIDN'T YOU HEAR ME CALLING YOU?

SMELLS SPEAK LOUDER THAN WORDS.

I SEE THAT YOUR MILLIE **TALKS** TO HER PLANTS!

LET'S TRY!

HEY, BABY, YOU ARE ONE **HOT** TOMATO! **LETTUCE KETCHUP** ON THE **LATEST** GARDEN GOSSIP!

CAN IT, TUNA-BREATH!

PLANTS CAN'T SHPEAK!

THEY'RE **TOO** SHTUPID

NOT AS **DUMB** AS THE **CAT** WHO TALKS TO THEM.

HEY! I'LL MATCH **WITS** WITH A GARDEN VEGETABLE **ANY** DAY OF THE **WEEK!**

76

COCK·A·DOODLE·**BOP**

WELL, SAY GOOD-BYE TO YOUR FARM BUDDIES. WE'RE HEADING **HOME**.

MOO.

HEE

HAW

PEEP

PEEP

PEEP

WHEN TRAVELING, IT'S WISE TO LEARN A FEW FOREIGN PHRASES.

WELL, SO LONG, BESSIE—PROMISE ME YOU'LL ALWAYS BE A HAPPY **COW**

...AND NOT SOME HAPPY MEAL.

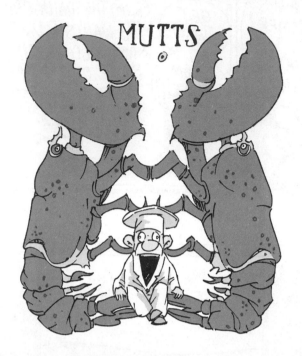

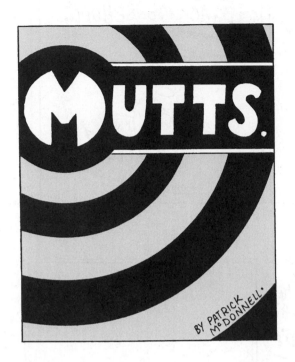

BACK TO WORK.

BACK TO SCHOOL.

BACK TO NORMAL.

HEY, MOOCH, WHAT'S THE **DIFFERENCE** BETWEEN THIS **GARBAGE** AND YOUR DRY CAT **FOOD**?

I DON'T **EAT** MY DRY CAT **FOOD**.

SNIFF
SNIFF
Z Z Z

SNIFF
SNIFF

HOW COME YOU CATS ARE ALWAYS "**SNIFFING**" PEOPLE'S BREATH?

TO MAKE SURE.

SURE OF **WHAT**!?!

THAT NOBODY'S BEEN AT MY **TUNA**.

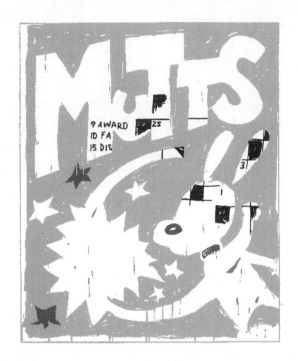

TIC
TIC
TIC
TIC
TIC

TIC
TIC
TIC
TIC

R·R·RING!

INTERNAL ALARM CLOCK.

ONCE AGAIN IT'S TIME TO TAKE WING AND HEAD SOUTH!

AHH, HOW ROMANTIC— TO FOLLOW YOUR HEART TO THE WARM SUN!

WELL... ACTUALLY I'M FOLLOWING MY STOMACH TO SOME TASTY BUGS.

KIND OF LOSES THE ROMANCE

EARL, MOOCH— I'M IN LOVE!

SHE'S JUST THE SWEETEST TWEETY I'VE EVER MET!

SHE SOUNDS SWELL.

YESH. DON'T LET THIS ONE GET AWAY.

WELL...

87

89

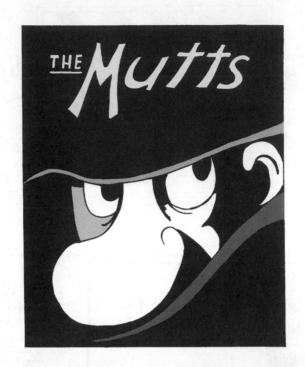

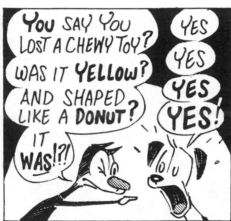

96

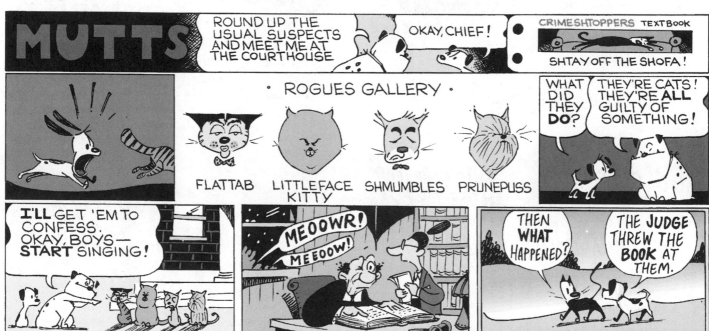

YOU WIN AGAIN,
YOU INSATIABLE
CRUEL FIEND!

CURSE YOU!
CURSE YOU!

CURIOSITY
CLAIMS
ANOTHER
INNOCENT
KITTY.

HELP! HELP!

IT'S USELESS—I'LL
NEVER ESHCAPE
THIS SEA OF SHEETS!
I'M DESTINED TO
JUST WASTE AWAY....
THE FORGOTTEN KITTY

... ALL
ALONE.

UMPF
ARG
AGGH!!!
MMMFF.

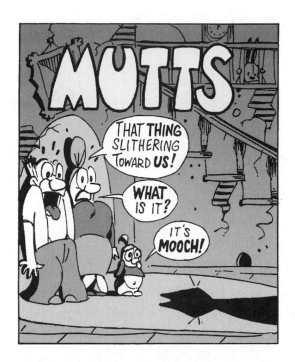

THE MORNING FOG SLOWLY LIFTS...

IF I DIED AND WENT TO HEAVEN

THEN

I MUST BE AN **ANGEL!**

AND ANGELS...

FLY!

K
L
U
N
K

...VERY SLOWLY.

I'M GOING TO NEED A **LOT** OF PRACTICE.

SO...

THIS IS...

HEAVEN.

YESH!

FATTY SNAX DELI

WOW! LOOK AT THIS FEAST! **THAT PROVES IT!** I DID DIE AND WENT TO **HEAVEN!**

HEY! WHO LET **YOU** IN!?!

LI'L ANGEL.

THE MORNING FOG...

123

WHAT DO YOU GET A GUY WHO HAS **EVERYTHING**!?! WHAT? WHAT? **WHAT**?

LET ME THINK... IF YOU HAD **EVERYTHING**... WHAT WOULD YOU **WANT**?...

...**NOTHING**!

YESH!

SHOPPING IS **SO MUCH EASIER** WHEN YOU MAKE A **LIST**.

GENIUS!

NOWADAYS WE ARE **ALL** BOGGED DOWN WITH **SHTUFF**. SHTUFF! **SHTUFF**! AND **MORE** SHTUFF!!! ACK! WE ARE ALL **SHTUFFOCATING**!!!

SO THIS HOLIDAY— I WILL GIVE THE **GIFT** OF...

...NOTHING.

I'M A **BIG** BELIEVER OF **PRACTICAL** PRESENTS.

I KNOW WHAT TO GET EARL— **ABSHOLUTELY** "**NOTHING**."

SALE

BUY BUY

ALTHOUGH AT **THIS** TIME OF YEAR IT SHMAY BE **HARD** TO FIND.

MORE! **MORE**!

BUY